T0085783

Deep-Sea Creatures

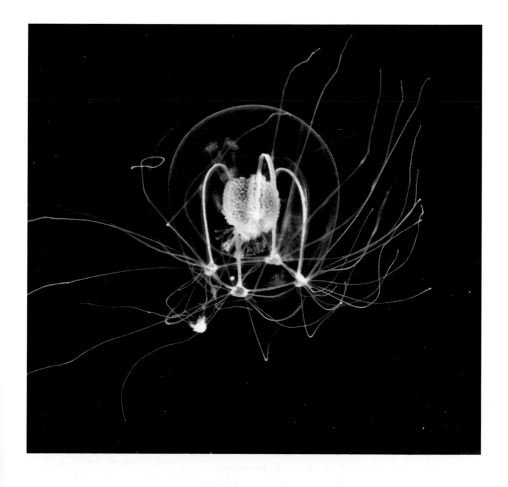

THIS EDITION
Editorial Management by Oriel Square
Produced for DK by WonderLab Group LLC
Jennifer Emmett, Erica Green, Kate Hale, *Founders*

Editors Grace Hill Smith, Libby Romero, Maya Myers, Michaela Weglinski;
Photography Editors Kelley Miller, Annette Kiesow, Nicole di Mella; **Managing Editor** Rachel Houghton;
Designers Project Design Company; **Researcher** Michelle Harris; **Copy Editor** Lori Merritt;
Indexer Connie Binder; **Proofreader** Larry Shea; **Reading Specialist** Dr. Jennifer Albro;
Curriculum Specialist Elaine Larson

Published in the United States by DK Publishing
1745 Broadway, 20th Floor, New York, NY 10019
Copyright © 2023 Dorling Kindersley Limited
DK, a Division of Penguin Random House LLC
23 24 25 26 10 9 8 7 6 5 4 3 2 1
001–334078–July/2023

A catalog record for this book
is available from the Library of Congress.
HC ISBN: 978-0-7440-7407-9
PB ISBN: 978-0-7440-7408-6

DK books are available at special discounts when purchased in bulk for sales promotions, premiums,
fundraising, or educational use. For details, contact: DK Publishing Special Markets,
1745 Broadway, 20th Floor, New York, NY 10019
SpecialSales@dk.com

Printed and bound in China

The publisher would like to thank the following for their kind permission to reproduce their images:
a=above; c=center; b=below; l=left; r=right; t=top; b/g=background

Alamy Stock Photo: Blue Planet Archive JMI 30b, Bluegreen Pictures / David Shale 20bc, Mark Conlin 16cr, Lee Dalton 18b,
Nature Picture Library 23br, Nature Picture Library / Alex Mustard 23t, Nature Picture Library / David Shale 15br,
Nature Picture Library / Wild Wonders of Europe / Lundgren 27br, Doug Perrine 20–21, Ted Small 16clb;
BluePlanetArchive.com: Phillip Colla 15cl, Espen Rekdal 8bl, David Wrobel 19tr; **Dreamstime.com:** 1621855 29b, Dibrova 8br,
Hotshotsworldwide 17tl; **Getty Images:** Image Source / Cultura RF / Alexander Semenov 1b, Moment / Sean Gladwell 3cb;
Getty Images / iStock: 3dsam79 13cr, E+ / Tammy616 4–5; **naturepl.com:** David Shale 24t, 28b, Wild Wonders of Europe /
Lundgren 26b, Solvin Zankl 12t; **NOAA:** Hidden Ocean 2005 Expedition: NOAA Office of Ocean Exploration / Kevin Raskoff 11,
NOAA / OAR / OER, 2016 Deepwater Wonders of Wake 22b, NOAA Okeanos Explorer Program, Our Deepwater Backyard 19b,
The NOAA Office of Ocean Exploration and Research, Deep-Sea Symphony 10bl; **Science Photo Library:** Dante Fenolio 9br, 25b;
Shutterstock.com: melissaf84 6br, OFC Pictures 7tr

Cover images: *Front:* **Alamy Stock Photo:** Lee Dalton bl; **Shutterstock.com:** Rich Carey, Julia Faranchuk tr;
Back: **Shutterstock.com:** Jacques Dayan cl

All other images © Dorling Kindersley
For more information see: www.dkimages.com

For the curious
www.dk.com

Deep-Sea
Creatures

Ruth A. Musgrave

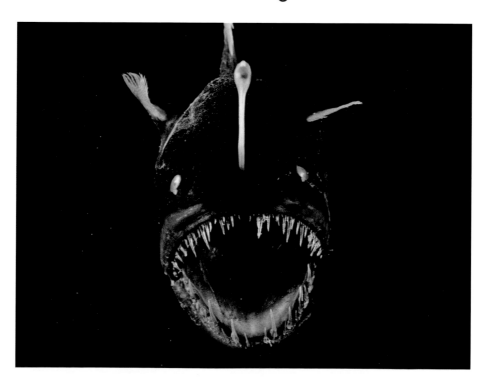

Contents

Let's Dive!

Welcome to Mission Deep-Sea Creatures. Some of the most amazing animals live deep in the ocean. Are you ready to get face-to-face with them?

You do not need swim fins or a snorkel. You need a research submersible for this adventure. Climb inside. Seal the hatch. Ready. Set.

Wait! There are a few things you should know. Diving to the deep is dangerous. It is dark and cold, and the weight of the ocean puts enormous pressure on your sub.

The Cold Deep
In the deep, the water temperature is 39°F (4°C) no matter where you are in the world.

Think of the ocean as having three levels. The top, the middle, and the bottom. You're going to the middle and bottom levels, which includes the twilight and midnight zones.

Sunlight starts to disappear as you sink in your sub. The sea goes from bright blue to darker and darker shades of blue. It finally turns gray and then black. That's because you are moving farther and farther away from the Sun.

Like all animals, deep-sea animals need to find food, avoid predators, and find mates. They just have to do it in the dark.

Ready? Set. Dive!

See-Through View

When the sunlight disappears, you have reached the beginning of the deep sea. That's about 600 feet (200 m) from the water's surface, or the height of four Statues of Liberty stacked on top of each other.

Look! What's that floating by? This jellyfish's body is transparent. That means clear, like glass.

Animals that live in the deep do not have trees, rocks, or anything else to hide behind. One of the best ways to hide is to be invisible.

Many fish, squid, jellyfish, shrimp, and other animals that live in the deep sea are transparent. Some are clear their whole life. Some are clear only when they are young. Young animals need any advantage they can get to avoid larger and faster predators.

Transparent animals do not have a lot of muscles. They are not fast or strong. Staying hidden in the dark is how they protect themselves.

See-Through Squid
Glass squid can be transparent. Like other squid, they can also change colors!

Camouflaging Colors

The two best colors for camouflage in the deep sea are black and red.

Black makes sense in the dark ocean, but how does the red color of this deep-sea jelly keep it hidden, too?

Most deep-sea animals cannot see the color red. Red looks black to them. That means the jelly disappears into the darkness.

Fish on the Move
Sea toads walk along the seafloor with their fins. They can force water out their gills to become jet-powered for a quick burst of speed.

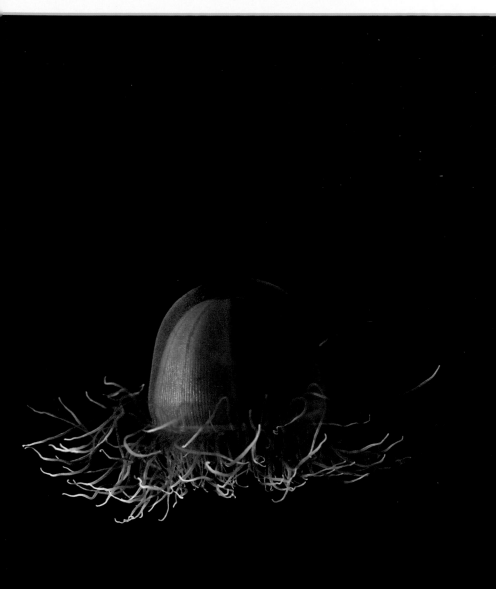

Hiding in the Light

Look up. You can still see a bit of light from the water's surface. If you look around, you will only see darkness. But the animals can see in the dark. They use that tiny bit of light that filters down from the surface.

Many ocean animals hunt by looking up. These predators use the surface light to see the shapes, shadows, and movements of animals above them. But some prey use the surface light to stay safe. These animals, like this firefly squid, make their own light that blends in with the light above.

Nine out of 10 deep-sea animals glow. They use light to hide, find food, avoid predators, and talk to each other.

Dimmer Switch

Many animals can also adjust the brightness of their glow, kind of like a lamp's dimmer switch. That way they can stay hidden and still move closer to, or farther from, the surface light.

lanternfish

That's a Lot of Jelly!

The sea is full of jellyfish and other kinds of jelly-like animals. Jellies do not have brains, bones, or hearts. Some are very small. Some stretch through the sea at extraordinary lengths.

One jelly-like animal is called a siphonophore. It is made up of many animals that are connected together. Each animal has a different role or job. Some catch food, some eat the food. Others help the siphonophore swim or protect it. They work together to survive. Now, that's some amazing teamwork!

Giant Jelly
Scientists observed a siphonophore that was estimated to be nearly 400 feet (122 m) long. If stretched in a straight line, it would be as long as four blue whales!

What's even more incredible? This jelly-like animal is delicate. Thousands of stinging tentacles hang from it. These tentacles catch whatever small animal bumps into them.

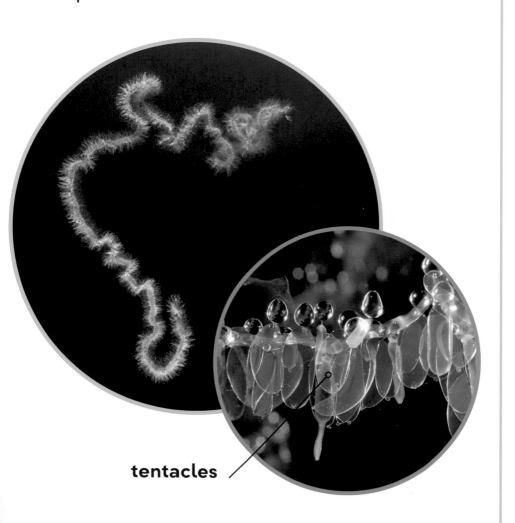

tentacles

Slime Time

Look at this slimeball. That's not an insult. It describes the disgustingly delightful hagfish.

When a shark or another fish tries to grab it, the hagfish oozes a thick slime. It releases gallons of it within a few seconds. The gooey mess clogs the predator's mouth, throat, and gills. The predator might be smothered in the slime if it doesn't let go of the hagfish.

Predators
Slime doesn't always save the hagfish! Elephant seals, whales, and penguins and other seabirds eat hagfish.

elephant seal

Hagfish are scavengers. They eat dead animals, often from the inside out. They tunnel through the mouth, gills, or body to get inside.

A hagfish uses its whole body to eat. It can tie its body into a knot. It rolls the knot down its body toward its mouth. The knot pushes against the food and helps the hagfish pull off chunks of flesh with its rows of teeth.

Dumbo Octopus

Steer the sub slowly.

You don't want to startle that small dumbo octopus. Giant fins on its head look like elephant ears. That's how it got its name. It flaps its big fins to swim.

There are many kinds of dumbo octopus. Most are 8 to 12 inches (20 to 30 cm) long. The longest is as tall as a human adult.

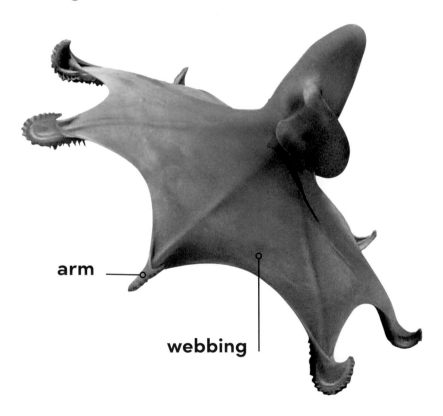

arm

webbing

Strong Suckers
This dumbo octopus has suckers on each arm. These suckers might be used to capture food.

Dumbo octopuses live deep in the sea. They hover near the seafloor, hunting worms and snails. They live as deep as 13,000 feet (3,962 m), making them one of the world's deepest-living octopuses.

Tricky Fish

What's a fishing pole doing down here? It's not a fishing pole. That lure is attached to an anglerfish. The lure tricks prey into swimming right up to the anglerfish's mouth. The anglerfish's body disappears into the dark water, but the tip of its lure glows. It looks like something to eat.

All Kinds of Anglers
There are more than 200 kinds of anglerfish.

lure

Only female anglerfish have a lure. The tiny male anglerfish looks nothing like a female.

The fish wiggles the glowing bait above its huge, toothy mouth. Hungry prey swim up for a nibble. The anglerfish gobbles up the prey.

Deep-Sea Sharks

About 500 kinds of sharks live throughout the world. More than half live in the deep sea.

Do you see that big shark just up ahead? That's a sixgill shark. This stocky shark is as long as three bicycles.

Some sharks that live closer to the water's surface visit the deep. The basking shark is the world's second-largest shark.

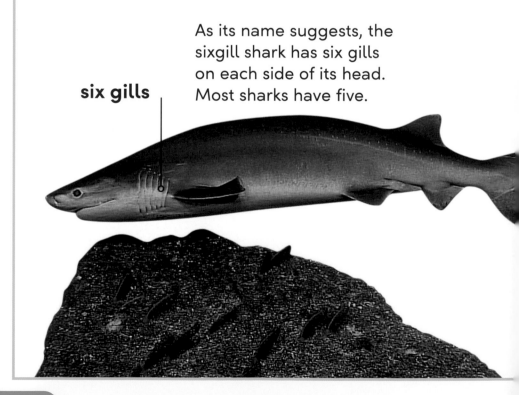

As its name suggests, the sixgill shark has six gills on each side of its head. Most sharks have five.

six gills

basking shark

The name describes its habit of basking, or floating, in the sun. But these sun-loving sharks also spend months diving deep to eat. Then, they return to the water's surface for the rest of the year.

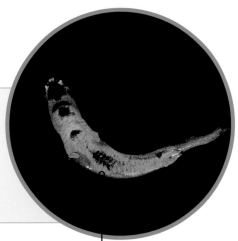

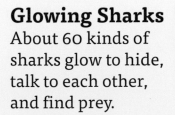

Glowing Sharks
About 60 kinds of sharks glow to hide, talk to each other, and find prey.

pygmy shark

A viperfish unhinges its jaw to open its mouth even wider to catch large prey.

Big Teeth

Look at the fish attached to those teeth! That's a viperfish. At 12 inches (30 cm) long, it is not big. But its teeth are gigantic! Finding food isn't easy in the deep. Once a predator finds prey, it must quickly catch and eat it before it gets away. Giant teeth help with this challenge.

A viperfish's sharp teeth are so long that they do not fit inside its mouth. After grabbing a fish, the viperfish closes its mouth as fast as it can. The teeth trap the prey inside, like a cage. The viperfish swallows its meal whole.

Sharp teeth help other deep-sea fish, like this fangtooth, catch meals, too.

Spooky in the Sea

What is that prowling just outside the sub's lights? Look at that big head and long, whip-like tail. It's a ghost shark! More than 50 kinds of ghost sharks live deep in the sea. They range in size from 24 to 79 inches (60 to 200 cm) long.

Ghost sharks are also called spookfish and rabbitfish.

They are not sharks but fish that are related to sharks and rays. Like sharks, a ghost shark's flexible skeleton is made of cartilage. That's the same material you have on the tip of your nose.

Special lines on their head and body feel movement in the water. This helps ghost sharks find their food. They use their flat teeth to crack open and eat crabs, mussels, and sea urchins.

Sharp Spines
Most ghost sharks have a venomous spine on their dorsal fin, which might help protect them from predators.

The Deepest Part of the Sea

Congratulations. You made it miles below the surface to the deepest part of the sea. It took a little more than two hours to get here.

Look at that ghostly creature. It is a snailfish. Its filmy fins and tail flow through the water as it searches for shrimp-like animals that live here. The snailfish finds one, quickly sucks it into its mouth, and then looks for more.

Scientists know very little about this part of the world. It is hard to get to or explore. But many spectacular animals live in the cold and dark depths of the ocean. Explorers discover something new every time they dive. There is still so much to learn. Is there another deep-sea mission in your future?

Deepest Divers
More people have made it to the top of Mount Everest, Earth's highest peak, than to the deepest part of the sea.

Glossary

Camouflage
A color, pattern, or behavior that helps an animal hide

Gills
The organs some ocean animals use to breathe

Octopus
An ocean animal with eight arms; related to squid

Predator
An animal that eats other animals

Prey
Animals that predators eat

Siphonophore
[SIE-fawn-a-for]
A jellyfish relative that is made up of many animals connected together

Squid
An ocean animal with eight arms and two tentacles; related to octopus

Submersible
An underwater vessel scientists use to explore the deep

Transparent
Clear or see-through, like glass

Water pressure
The force of the weight of water

Index

Quiz

Answer the questions to see what you have learned. Check your answers in the key below.

1. Why is red a good color for camouflage in the deep sea?

2. True or False: See-through fish swim in the ocean.

3. How does a hagfish protect itself?

4. Name two kinds of sharks found in the deep sea.

5. How does a dumbo octopus swim?

6. How does an anglerfish attract its food?

7. How do ghost sharks find their food?

8. How does a siphonophore catch food?

1. It looks black to most deep-sea animals 2. True 3. It releases slime 4. Basking shark and sixgill shark 5. It flaps its fins 6. With a glowing lure 7. Special lines on their head and body feel movement in the water 8. With its tentacles